I0766936

STANFORD SPIRIT

The stories, passions and dreams of
32 Stanford students

collected and edited by

Jason Shen '08

ISBN: 978-1-84728-595-9

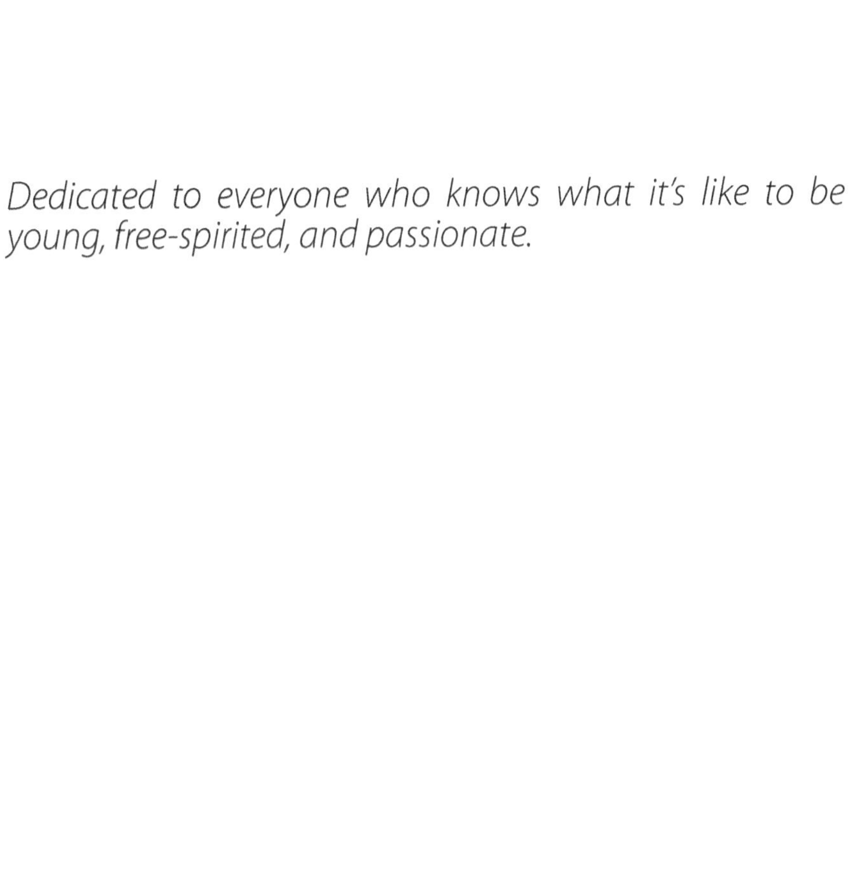

Dedicated to everyone who knows what it's like to be young, free-spirited, and passionate.

Acknowledgments

There is no way this book could have happened without the help of Laure Negiar '07. When I read her article in the Stanford Daily called "Stanford, It's All About the People." I knew I had found a kindred soul. She helped make this book a reality in many ways.

I am indebted to my girlfriend for all her help with the book layout and design, copy editing, and photography. Also for all the love and morale support. We make a great team.

I want to thank everyone who wrote for the book. Sorry about all the spam emails! It's been incredible to read the entries as they came into my inbox. I made a promise that this book would get published because these stories, passions and dreams are most definitely worth sharing.

James Gwartney, Richard L. Stroup, Dwight Lee, I am so glad you three economists decided to team up and write a book called *Common Sense Economics: What Everyone Should Know About Wealth and Prosperity*. The concept of the "comparative advantage" is what first got me thinking about making this book in the first place. It's also just a great introduction to economics.

Finally, I want to thank my mom and dad: Shixin Mao and Anping Shen. They are outstanding parents who have worked hard to make sure I got an excellent education and told me to believe in my dreams. I love you and thank you for loving me.

INTRODUCTION

When I am asked what the best part of going to Stanford is, I always say, "the people." And by that I mean the staff, faculty, and especially the students. I love Stanford students. I mean there are a few jerks and bores here and there but for the most part, we are just unbelievable. You feel it the minute you get here.

Freshman year was so exciting because you were constantly meeting new people. And everyone seemed so cool, so nice and so *normal*. Then a week or a month after meeting them you would find out that they had volunteered to build a 10-story low income home <C.H. 09>, or competed in the Olympics, or won a nationwide piano competition <E.K. 08>, or traveled to exotic locales <Peter Derman 07, Laure Negiar 07>. It can put a quick damper on a big ego.

The seed for this book was planted the summer after freshman year. I was reading a book on economics that talked about leveraging your "comparative advantage". I figured mine is coming up with crazy ideas, so I had the idea of a book written by Stanford students. I wrote it down and by the time school started I had forgotten about it. As sophomore year rolled on, I felt like I wasn't meeting as many new people as freshman year. Which made me think of the book idea. Maybe I could meet new people if I made a book about Stanford students, by Stanford students. And so *Stanford Spirit* was born.

I would get students to write short entries about themselves. How could I capture an entire person in such few words? I would give them prompts that summed up the human experience. That is, their past, present and future. After a fair amount of brainstorming, I settled on "I remember", "I live for/to", and "I would like to" as the three prompts for people to share their stories, passions and dreams.

When I pitched this book idea to people, many responded, "Oh, that sounds like a great idea. I don't think I have anything good to write, but I would love to read it." Now I understand where these people are coming from, but I have to disagree. I think everyone has something to share, they just need to find their voice.

Maybe it's because people here are modest. Look at how <Anonymous 08> treats her acceptance letter. But I'm sure that can't be the whole reason because then there is <Eli Alcaraz 08>.

Stanford University itself could write an entry for this book. After all, it was founded on the memory of a son who died before his time. It exists to "qualify students for personal success and direct usefulness to life" (Founder's Grant). And it is not afraid to dream. It is not afraid to "outgrow old thoughts and ways and dare to think on new lines" (Jane Stanford).

I love that last sentence. Jane Stanford helped the University thrive for 10 years after the death of her husband, Leland Stanford. This school was born innovative and progressive. It was coed when most universities accepted only men. GPS was invented here. Google and Ebay headquarters are a town over. In the society we live in today, the road to success is more unpredictable than ever. Stanford is not hampered by long traditions, which allows it to grow and excel in unexpected ways. Like Stanford students do.

It is the dreams of our students that excites me most. So many of the entries talk about making a contribution, changing the world for the better and just living life fully. It's been challenging and at times frustrating to put this book together, but I feel hopeful and inspired whenever I browse through this collection of student entries. I hope it touches you in the same way. Go Card!

Jason Shen '08

August 13, 2006

MEET THE STANFORD SPIRIT WRITERS

Each person in this book comes from a different background. Each hails from a different part of the globe, grew up in different circumstances and has different talents, abilities and beliefs. But we all hold one thing in common. We were accepted into and attended this great institution known as Leland Stanford Junior University. We've all got some Stanford spirit in us.

The stats

Males - 12	2009 - 7	2008 - 14
Females- 16	2007 - 4	2006 - 4
Anonymous - 3	Anonymous - 2	

The names (in book order)

Sarah Victor 2008	M.O. 2009
Eli Alcaraz 2008	Nate Downs 2006
Anonymous 200?	Marisa Dowling 2009
C.H. 2009	E.K. 2008
Laure Negiar 2007	Peter Derman 2007
Rafael Zuzuarregui 2006	H.Z. 2009
Elspeth Olson 2008	N.J. 2008
ZiHan Lin 2008	Stedman Wilson 2006
S.L. 2008	L.G. 2008
Alice Lee 2009	A.P. 2009
S.A. 2006	M.A.K. 2008
Anonymous 2008	Leah Sawyer 2007
Jae Won Joh 2009	Abby Zeitlin 2008
Therin Jones 2009	Maribel Diaz 2008
Jessica Haro 2007	Jason Shen 2008
Takeo Rivera 2008	Anonymous 200?

SARAH VICTOR
2008

I REMEMBER GETTING INTO STANFORD.

I got in from the waitlist, and I'm not afraid to say it! I had already agonized through my choices, waiting until May 1 to make my final decision - Dartmouth. The weather may suck, but Dartmouth has one of the best college debate teams in the country, and I wanted to pursue that activity in college. I joined the Dartmouth 08 mailing list, checked their message boards, sent in my deposit, and proudly wore my Dartmouth shirt to school.

In mid-May, that all changed. I got a phone call from Stanford, asking me if I still wanted to be on the waitlist. Sure, why not? The woman then asked me whether or not I would likely come to Stanford if taken off the waitlist. I said, truthfully, "I'd have to think about it." According to my mom, this was the wrong answer. "They'll never take you off the waitlist now! They'll give it to someone who really wants to go there!"

Turns out she was wrong. A few days later I got an (albeit delayed) acceptance letter in the mail, and the process started all over again. I still have the spreadsheet I created to compare Dartmouth and Stanford! While I had accepted Dartmouth, I realized I wouldn't be nearly as happy there as I would be at Stanford. I'm so glad I made the choice I did - the right choice for me. Stanford Class of 2008!

Sarah Victor 2008

I LIVE FOR THE CHANCE TO TALK

with my family. For the times when my dad sends me emails he thinks are really, really funny, but are only mildly so. For the times when he sends me the same email twice. For the times he rambles on about something I already know, but I listen because I want a chance to be with him.

For the emails my grandma sends me with bright red text (sometimes on a yellow background). For the risque forwards she passes along. For the way she writes me like we're sitting right next to each other.

For the text messages my brother sends me from school about his witty comments to my old teachers. For the times when I say "I love you, bye" and he just says "Bye" back, but I know he loves me too and he's just being a teenage boy. For all the times he's called me ugly and I've called him stupid, and we both know we don't really mean it.

For the messages from my mom that begin with "Hi sweetie!" For the care packages that are random, but always adorable. For the way we can still gossip even though we are thousands of miles away.

For the connections that won't break down over time or distance.

Sarah Victor 2008

I WOULD LIKE TO MAKE A DIFFERENCE.

I want somebody to grow up and come back to me and say, "Thank you so much for what you have done; you've changed my life." I want to help people. I want to be the person that so many people have been for me throughout my life. I would like to have kids someday, to see them grow up to become amazing people. I would like a profession where I could interact with people every day. I want a job where I can teach (not necessarily in the strictest sense of the word), but where I can also learn from the people around me.

Sarah Victor 2008

ELI ALCARAZ
2008

I REMEMBER WHEN I GOT INTO STANFORD.

That had been my dream since like the age of 9. I didn't know why I wanted to go; only that Stanford was where I was meant to be. I wanted nothing more than to do gymnastics here. I would periodically become stressed and anxious because I thought I wasn't doing the right things to get in.

Well, March finally came, and I knew they mailed the letters out on a Monday. On Wednesday I was leaving for a competition and would not be back home until Sunday. I knew the information that would change the next four years of my life would come while I was gone. I also knew that my mother would be home and receive it first, so that meant I couldn't call because I would be able to tell in her voice if I got in and I needed to do well at the meet. So, I planned on not talking to my mom for the next four days.

When we had just put our suitcases in the room my dad got a call, he said it was for me. I got on the phone and my mom was screaming and crying, she was yelling, "You got in, you got in, I'm sorry but I had to open it, it said 'Congratulations' on the front." I was so happy I yelled at my teammate that I was going to Stanford next year and gave him the hardest high five I have ever given. I was so happy that life didn't matter. I will remember March 31st for the rest of my life.

Eli Alcaraz 2008

I LIVE FOR COMPETITION;

I don't like losing. That is not to say I don't know how to lose, but that I do all in my power to ensure victory. I made bets all the time during gymnastics practice, like on who could perform a new skill first. At the beginning, I lost a lot of bets, but it taught me how to make myself win, against all odds. It got to a point during my club career where I would never lose a bet. It didn't matter if I had never made the skill before; I would make it.

It taught me the meaning of the saying, "They can do it because they believe they can." Many times, the only reason I would win was because losing was not an option. Competition was no longer a gamble, it was something I dominated. Competition excites me, it carries over into all other aspects of life. I live to write the best story and competition is a theme that will carry the entire book. Life is an All-Around competition and I am here to win it.

I WOULD LIKE TO GET TO A STAGE

in life where I get free stuff wherever I go. Like the way a movie star gets free meals when they go to a restaurant because everyone saw them eat there and thus business will go up. Or how a celebrity gets free clothes because people will look at them and want the clothes.

I would like to reach that stage where I get things for free. I would still work and have a job, but for me, I value things I get for free far more than things I pay for. I take excellent care of the things I pay for because I want to get the most bang for my buck, but there is just something about getting free stuff that is so cool.

Eli Alcaraz 2008

ANONYMOUS
200?

I REMEMBER SWIMMING WITH SEALS

down at Hopkins Marine Station under the excuse of conducting pinniped kinesiology. I had been in the water for four hours one day, and my entire body had begun to go numb, when I suddenly heard a wet "blrmph!" from behind me. I whirled around, but nothing was there. I paused, certain that I had started hallucinating, when again, directly behind me, I heard the "blrmph! blrmph!" Again. I whirled around in the water one more time, and again--nothing.

In my panic, I dropped my underwater camera, and as I fumbled to catch it, I saw two young bulls swimming figure-8's between my legs. I got very still--being that close to the seals reminded me that they could break a 2x4 in half without really trying. I lost sight of one of the bulls, and again, I heard the "blrmph!" sound in back of me.

This time I didn't move at all. Suddenly, the seal behind me reached around my waist with his flippers and gave me what was most definitely the equivalent of a seal-hug. I tried to gently turn around to look the bull in face, but as I moved, I felt him swim away and saw his friend dash into the kelp forest. I remember having to stay in the water for another hour to make sure that I could re-trace every detail and emotion, so that when people asked me about the coolest thing that had ever happened to me, I could perfectly remember that moment.

On a rather unfortunate note, I found out a few days later that young bulls have been known to "hug" their fair share of idle swimmers... it is due not to a need to communicate with their fellow mammals, but rather, it is a way for them to release their pent-up sex drive.

Anonymous 200?

I LIVE FOR THE BEAUTY

excitement and peace that comes to me
when I discover something new.

Anonymous 200?

I WOULD LIKE TO LIVE A GOOD, HONEST

and whole life, with many dogs--one of which will be a Goldendoodle. I like dogs--a lot....especially Goldendoodles, the Dog of the Future. I am going to own four dogs throughout my life. Brutus will be a harlequin great dane. Hermes will be my Goldendoodle. Fitzwilliam will be my standard poodle. And Killer will be my westie. Killer will come later in my life so that I can haul him around in my giant, granny carpet bag. He will wear mini Fair Isle sweaters that will match the giant swaths of old-lady blanket-sweaters that I plan on wearing at all times. I might start out with Fitzwilliam, but Brutus could also be a possibility, depending on where I live and how much money I have after I graduate.

Anonymous 200?

C. H.
2009

I REMEMBER THE WORK AND THE REWARD.

Backbreaking labor, converting a ten-story building in Seattle from offices to low-income housing. Sledgehammers, bricks, aching muscles, bruises, asbestos, sexism and racism within the construction industry. Hardly the "proper" post-high school job for a five-foot-three Chinese-American girl living in suburbia, but then, I have always preferred feeling out-of-place to being pigeonholed in stereotypes, disheartening as it may be to never-quite-belong.

The reward for my months of toil was also a way of challenging assumptions, those of society, school, my parents, myself: ten months of traveling and volunteering abroad. I remember irrigating 10,000 grape plants on an organic farm in Australia and catching glimpses of wild kangaroos in the bush. I remember petting tigers in Thailand, washing an elephant in Nepal, speaking in the common language of pictures and gestures and gifts to a monk in Tibet. From living and teaching in Shanghai for five months, I remember the joy of discovering my family, and the pain of losing my uncle to cancer.

With eyes and mind and heart wide open to everything around me, I remember most of all the unfettered freedom to think, feel, and really live.

C.H. 2009

I LIVE FOR CONNECTING WITH PEOPLE

around the world, and empowering myself through new experiences that are usually dreaded at first, though rarely regretted afterwards. Also: cuddly animals, swimming under waterfalls, music, never-ending conversations, nonsensical but somehow hilarious jokes, the smell of books, and so many other splendors of this world.

I WOULD LIKE TO DO AN INFINITE LIST

of too many things (alleviate poverty and injustice, travel the world, study the human brain, learn to sing, etc etc). So really I would just like to learn to be satisfied with the moment, to act in the present more than I dream about the future, to make positive changes in the world, however humble (and perhaps also to use fewer clichés).

LAURE NEGIAR
2007

I REMEMBER ALL THE GREAT TRIPS

I've taken with my family. My parents have always thought that traveling is one of the most valuable things in life. They traveled all over the world before they even had a VCR, a car, or any of the other modern 'necessities.' After my three younger siblings and I were born, they always took us with them. One year, when I was in tenth grade, we saw five different continents (Europe, North America, Asia, Australia, and Africa). Sometimes when I tell people about our trips I'm afraid they'll think I'm bragging, but I'm not. I just get really excited thinking about them. I'm incredibly grateful to my parents for taking us on these trips, which have allowed me to see beautiful places and wonderful people and to think of issues from the Other's perspective.

Trips have also been the best bonding experiences for my family. Especially now that I'm living in a different country than my family, being able to spend time exploring new places with them is one of the things that have kept us really close. Even after several months during which I've not seen my parents or my siblings, I always feel just as comfortable with them as I always have. Inevitably, at several points during our travels, we get lost, and my parents and sister always react in the same way. While we're lost it's not especially amusing, but in retrospect it's very entertaining.

My father, who usually got us lost in the first place because he wanted to show us the "real" , "local", "typical" places, denies that we're lost, insists that he will manage to get us to our destination, and in trying to do so generally gets us even more lost, especially since he refuses to rely on maps. My mother gets quite upset, because, in her own words, she "hates to wander about aimlessly." At the height of the crisis my oldest sister bursts out laughing and can't stop and the rest of us kids join in, which only increases tension between my mother and father. Eventually we end up finding the place we were looking for and all is forgotten; the incident becomes nothing more than a funny memory.

Laure Negiar 2007

I LIVE FOR AS OF RIGHT NOW,

two main things: learning as much as possible, and the people I love. I know I won't be in school forever, so I want to accumulate as much knowledge as possible while I can. Learning obviously doesn't have to stop when you leave school, but I'll have so much less time to learn later.

Right now my time is pretty much divided between only two things: schoolwork and fun. I don't have to worry about taking care of my house or my kids or any of the burdens of adult life. I'm scared that I won't be able to keep my brain challenged as it is now, because I love the feeling that my mind is constantly expanding.

Learning is only one of the things I live for, though. Some of my greatest joys come from being and doing things with my friends and family. They don't even have to be big things: a great conversation over dinner or coffee, knowing that you will be understood and not judged, knowing that you can trust the other person and confide in them; a tennis match; a barbeque on a warm spring evening. When the two come together - being with friends and learning - it's pure happiness.

I WOULD LIKE TO WORK AT THE TOP

levels of government, and I've wanted that ever since I was a little kid. I've been warned that working in government is not what you think it is, that I'll be frustrated and that I'll come running back to the private sector. But if I don't give it a shot, I know I'll regret it for the rest of my life, so I'm going to try.

RAFAEL ZUZUARREGUI
2006

I REMEMBER MY FIRST WEEK AT STANFORD

and how excited I was to meet all the new faces. I came onto the campus as a freshman not knowing a single person and ready to build new friendships and reconstruct my ideals and values. As I moved into the dorm, I remember seeing the room doors open and people getting settled in; Corcoran had his sound board out with all of his audio equipment tossed everywhere in the room. DJ Elusive also had his whole audio station set up already and Preble was making his bed.

As I walked into my room, my roommate Steve Dewitt had already moved in and had his side of the room set up. We introduced ourselves to each other in that slightly awkward excitement that comes with the novelty of moving into a new phase of life with a friend you've never met before. My parents helped me unload and it was then that I began my new life at Stanford.

Now, looking back, those guys are still my friends and we still laugh about the same things, about the burping in the bathroom that would go on for hours, Rob's girl problems and who Coxx would come back to the dorm with after a frat party. I remember the glory of those Burbank days and how much fun we had. I wish life mirrored that at all stages.

Rafael Zuzuarregui 2006

I LIVE TO SEEK HOW GOD FITS INTO

my life. In our PC society, I think religion has become sort of taboo, something that will offend people, and spirituality is seen as more acceptable because it's more personal and carries less negative connotation with it. My experience at college has been enriched so much by trying to figure out how God fits into my life and how I would try to mirror God's presence in my own life. I've stumbled and haven't been perfect, but I've grown by acknowledging that and striving to better myself in the image of God. That is the beauty of the Christian life, I think. The fact that we acknowledge our greatest weakness as humans, the inability to love one another completely, and still are able to look at each other with grace and forgiveness and continue to walk along side one another on the path of life is something powerful. I hope that through interacting with me, people are able to see a glimpse of God's love. That's what I live for, sharing God's love with others despite my own imperfections.

Rafael Zuzuarregui 2006

I WOULD LIKE TO BE A MAN

that people remember for his respect of others and for trying to love them as best he could. When I come back to Stanford, or even return to high school, I don't want people to remember me for my hobbies or activities I was associated with, but I want the memory of how I acted towards them and treated them to stand out above all.

Rafael Zuzuarregui 2006

ELSPETH OLSON
2008

I REMEMBER THE WAY MY HEART STOPPED

and plummeted into my stomach the first time I had a solo. I remember how I knew, the moment before the choir director pointed at me, that it was my turn to take it.

I remember the intense pride of a dream fulfilled when I had a solo in front of at least a hundred alumni of my choir, and I remember the dazzling, dreamlike feeling of an individual bow with applause just for me.

Elspeth Olson 2008

I LIVE FOR THE GOOSEBUMP-

inducing exhilaration of wind, rain, and the brilliant contrasts of color in the world.

Elspeth Olson 2008

I WOULD LIKE TO FIND A JOB

where I can work with people who understand that "good enough" is not good enough. People who strive for excellence and know that it's not about actually achieving excellence. I would like to find out what it is I'm specially good at.

Elspeth Olson 2008

ZIHAN LIN
2008

I REMEMBER WHEN I WAS JUST A WEE-BIT

in China, would have never imagined that one day I would be studying at a renowned college in the future. Hell, I never imagined studying in the future, period. Those days of Transformers, DragonballZ, and Sonic - all in Chinese - were the great days of ignorance and bliss. The day I touched down in LA, I had no idea I would be living here. Mommy gave me the impression of "we're just visiting daddy." Liar. Just kidding, Mom.

But even when I applied for college, Stanford was still a vague concept - it's some decent school laying around up north somewhere. Yep, that was back then, the past tense, the before and uneducated. When my life was easily determined by the whim of my own mind. When school was easy because rote memorization is how you ace tests. When things weren't REAL yet. When I relied on parents for room and board. When that big package from Stanford had not arrived from the mail...

ZiHan Lin 2008

I LIVE FOR INNOVATIVE THINKING.

Forming a company has always been a dream of mine, but what to do? Since I have gotten here, that part has really come alive. Entrepreneurship running crazy everywhere. Talks, symposiums, seminar series, dinners, networking, socials, yada yada yada - I live for those because they lead to "potentially"s. A single connection can potentially get something started which can turn my life around in ways I would never imagine, or so I hear from all these talks. Yeah, I want to be in the spotlight. I want to be moving. I want to be innovative and thinking about how to make that green. I live for it. One idea after another - that's how I would like to do it. A checklist maybe - a big long checklist of company-opening ideas to get through. A list of great ideas helping billions and making bajillions.

ZiHan Lin 2008

I WOULD LIKE TO TO FOLLOW THE SCENT

of my own interest and let it lead me to somewhere rich and powerful. My view of life is not like standardized testing - there is more than one way to do well. In the future, I would like to collaborate and cooperate with friends and family. A coporation built around my connections is what I imagine. The recognition received wherever I go would be ideal but at least let me be conscious of a world of happiness because I, ZiHan Lin, did something. I want people to be so happy that I started this.. THING.. that they are willing to fly me to China, buy me In-N-Out, send me t-shirts, pay my rent, give me a house as a gift. Some day that goal will be achieved, and that some day will come - first in my dreams then in my actions.

S. L.
2008

I REMEMBER STANDING IN

Tiananmen square.   My classmates and I were scattered across it in groups, marveling at the sheer vastness of the space, while sweating in the intense heat. Around us, dozens of hawkers held up perspiring bottles of water, a live demonstration of perfect competition. It took us awhile to realize that most of the bottles' plastic cap-seals were broken.

As I scanned the crowds of tourists milling and smiling for photos, I found it difficult to believe that a mere fifteen years earlier, this vast concrete sea was packed with students, standing up for their beliefs, only to be rolled over by indifferent tanks. The regularly spaced sign posts politely asking visitors to keep off the grass possessed an unsettling cordiality, their wooden panels appearing more humane than government men in uniform of the past.

I   LIVE   FOR   BREAKING   OUT   OF

my timid shell and bursting into mind-boggling antics. And for the puzzled expressions on people's faces, followed by bursts of giggles, chuckles and laughs, because I am led to believe that I've somehow increased the level of happiness in their day by one mmHg.

I live for making nerdy jokes about love only being heightened levels of dopamine in the sunshine. For losing myself in a divinely rich chocolate souffle. For stalking campus-damned furry creatures called squirrels with my Cybershot in an effort to prove that they really are adorable. For enjoying this paradise I somehow had the good luck of stumbling upon without ever visiting it or joining the groups of tourists who gawk at real Stanford students in their natural habitat. For being able to gawk along with them at my peers and wonder at the amazing specimens surrounding me. For having others question my close-minded theories and being forced to admit that I was wrong, but also realizing I can still learn from my blatant errors. For the beauty of a freshly tuned piano. For having friends who teach me to laugh at myself and who let me punch them back. For feeling like this textbox couldn't possibly encompass or keep up with my neurons firing in response to the prompt.

I WOULD LIKE TO SAMPLE EVERYTHING

in this buffet called Life. (Forgive this ridiculously cliché metaphor but most would agree that it fits me.) I want to taste every fungi, savor every sauce, smack my lips on deep fried stuff, and close my eyes at wondrous green leafy things. I want to slurp, sip, chomp, nibble, and gnaw. I want to sigh in bliss or pop up in my seat with surprise. I won't mind feeling nauseous (so long as it isn't due to food poisoning) because I will have at least tried it. I don't ever want to feel satiated but want to always have a slight ache of hunger so that my palate can experience new textures, my olfactory sensors encounter novel aromas, my eyes rest upon previously unknown edible terrains. And finally, I want to make the kitchen my own so that I might replicate the buffet for others with some of my own original flavors.

ALICE LEE
2009

I   REMEMBER   DRESSING   UP

in a pink frilly dress, putting on my mom's yellow clip-on earrings, and tying my hair into two tight buns--all to pose for the family camera. Dress-up for me was serious business. I modeled my little self down the narrow hallway of our Nugent Dr. house, princess-waving to an imaginary crowd. Although only my eyes were sparkling diamonds that day, I had this dream to keep me entertained throughout childhood. I remember sitting by the Mickey Mouse wading pool, dipping my tiny toes in as my brother and I ate watermelon, competing to see who could spit seeds out the farthest. I remember traveling —20 hour plane rides to Taiwan, 10 hour drives to Atlanta, 30 trips around the world in daydreams. I remember Logan, the best babysitter in the universe, wheeling us in the world's finest red jeep down the sidewalk to my best friend's house. I remember celebrating every year with her because we had the same birthdays and were convinced we were twins. And most of all, I remember my grandpa's smiling face in the hospital, before he left this earth forever.

Alice Lee 2009

I LIVE TO HELP PEOPLE.

I am alive because others are dying; I am too fortunate, too elevated, too privileged. Why do I get to go to Stanford? Well, I do. And with that, I of all people should be the one to devote my time and energy for the less fortunate. I live for community service, for education, for young kids' dreams. I live to spread Master Cheng Yen's love in Tzu Chi, to plan fellowships for Alpha Phi Omega, to build houses for Habitat for Humanity. I live to study biology and become a doctor, for free humanitarian clinics in third-world countries. I live to collect wristbands in support of different causes; I want the rainbow on my arm to represent my love for peace.

Alice Lee 2009

I WOULD LIKE TO PASS THE MCATS

first and foremost. Then survive residency. Then open my own clinic, in an East Asian country. I want to master the language of Chinese so I can satisfy my parents and communicate with my patients. I would like to start a business, hire people, own a company--where all profit goes to bettering others. I would like to be well-known in my line of work, to be recognized for my efforts, to make lots of moolah. I would like to be a home-owner, a good wife, a great mom, and a friendly neighbor. Lastly, I want to give back to Stanford, the majestic institution that inspired it all.

S. A.
2006

I REMEMBER, AND CAN NEVER FORGET,

when the poet Li Young Lee told us on the first day of class to write the whole urgent truth, to write the poem like the Death Angel's sword were at our neck, and to write for life, because we only have one life. And then he brought out a big white tome with JUNG written across the cover and I knew this man would change my life.

I LIVE FOR FINDING INNER TRUTH

and authenticity in myself and others. I live for art and poetry and music and creativity. I love people who can laugh as much as they cry and I believe that the risk it takes to remain in the bud is greater than the risk it takes to blossom, but I can't remember who said that...

I WOULD LIKE TO BE A POET

and filmmaker and creative/socially conscious
entrepreneur. I would like to travel and scuba
dive in shipwrecks and find treasures wherever
I go.

S.A. 2006

ANONYMOUS
2008

I REMEMBER THE MOMENT WHEN

I got the acceptance letter... and not understanding that something like this could happen to me. Unfortunately, instead of feeling that MY WORTH had risen to the level of Stanford's excellence... I felt that Stanford's excellence was tarnished by accepting me.

I LIVE TODAY SO I CAN LIVE TOMORROW.

In my world, that means that my life is about delayed gratification. I have a bizarre amount of self-control and ambition… to the extent that sometimes it scares me. I don't know why I have so much ambition, but I fear that it's not for the right reasons.

I WOULD LIKE TO BE

a social revolutionary.

JAE WON JOH
2009

I REMEMBER WATCHING SESAME STREET

in Japan. I remember thinking it would be so cool to be able to go to America and learn English. There I was, 5 years old, a Korean boy living in Japan, already wanting to be ambitious and pick up my third language. And then my parents announced to me that we were moving to America. Heck if I remember the original reason why. But we did. I didn't even know what college was back then; I don't think I had even heard of the word at that point. But look at me now. Over a dozen years later I'm here at Stanford. Just goes to show how random things can be sometimes, I guess.

I remember all those nights I spent staying up late to finish homework and double-check it, because of course I had to do well in school. By the time I was in sixth grade sleeping around midnight or 1AM wasn't entirely uncommon. Yeah, I've been called the god of nerds before. I remember the projects, the friends I will probably never see again, the ridicule at the little yellow boy who struggled with English, the ghetto neighborhood where my family and I first lived, and where we had parts of our already pathetic first car stolwen, I remember the teachers who were patient and the teachers who resorted to yelling at the first sign of trouble. I remember my first of many crushes--a cute little girl in first grade who had the sweetest smile.

I remember my first all-nighter. Nothing clearly really, as memories like that tend to be, but I do remember that I remembered nothing of the next school day after it was over, when I crashed like a meteor into my bed. I remember all those crazy moments filling out college applications thinking that in my hands I held the future of the next four years. I pulled all-nighter after all-nighter during my winter break, hoping to perfect them. Eh, who cares now, but to my successors, I gotta say, more power to ya. I'd sure as heck never want to go through all that again.

I remember my first day at Stanford. I was pumped up like a ninja. It's had its ups and downs, but overall it's been pretty spectacular. Heh, quite a long ways I've come, now that I think about it.

Jae Won Joh 2009

I LIVE TO JUST ENJOY LIFE, REALLY.

I look outside and I see beauty, in a classic sense. Call me Zen, call me a dreamer, call me a philosopher, whatever. My stress level is lower than yours will ever be. Might well live longer than you, who knows. But I hafta admit, I love the craziness of life, too. I love the bustle of life that I feel. I live for all the crazy studying I have to pull, all the attempts to shine, all the friends that I work and mess around with. I live for the thrill of having done something and done it well--I just happen to like balancing work and play.

Jae Won Joh 2009

I WOULD LIKE TO TEACH.

More than anything I'd like to teach at a university, where I can always be at the forefront of what is happening, and also do my own research, maybe even forming a company out of an idea. And I'll do anything to make that dream come true, bit by bit. Living a dream? Why not? It's a short life we all live, and you might as well live it doing what you want most.

THERIN JONES
2009

I REMEMBER KAYAKING THE BRISTOL

Channel with a rosy-cheeked Norwegian on my right and a towering Russian on my left on Welsh afternoons. Kissing a Mexican boy, marked already for deportment, on his forehead, then his nose, then his lips. Climbing the squatting willow tree in my childhood backyard after years of being intimidated by its shadow against my bedroom windowpane at dusk. Getting the flu as a child and wishing to die for the first time. Curling up in my room after lonely, middle school bus rides and regretting my hairstyle, my braces, my bony elbows. The sting of alienation when returning home for the first time after having "studied abroad."

I LIVE FOR MY COUNTRY.

I live to offer everything I have to everything that has made me. I live to write and absorb and learn and grow. I specify that I want to grow like a tree rather than bacteria, which my sister claims is faster and "better," because a tree reaches while never losing its roots. I want to flower and realize it as it happens.

I WOULD LIKE TO ECHO FOREVER.

I would like to travel, learn to break dance, build a skateboard, and drive a stick shift car for longer than a "trial period." I would like to witness a birth, grow a piece of fruit, and fly a plane.

Therin Jones 2009

JESSICA HARO
2007

I REMEMBER WHEN I LEARNED

when to jump during "All Right Now," a true freshman rite of passage. It was in the middle of the quad at the end of the band run during New Student Orientation. I was full of energy, surrounded by new friends, and excited to start my first year at Stanford. Five, six, seven, eight, woo!

Jessica Haro 2007

I LIVE TO DANCE.

There is a freedom that only dance can bring, whether it's on stage or on the dance floor. Flamenco was my first passion and remains one of my greatest loves. I feel the rhythm deep within me; it makes me feel alive in a way nothing else can. To be on stage, under the lights, in front of an audience, expressing pure emotion - this, to me, is to live.

Jessica Haro 2007

I WOULD LIKE TO CHANGE THE FACE

of the teen magazine industry by creating something positive.

TAKEO RIVERA
2008

I REMEMBER PRESSING A CELL PHONE

against my freshman ear around 10pm because that's when I'd get free minutes. My dad is on the other line telling me about Rivera men. About legacy. About how it would be a shame that my grandfather came from the Philippines penniless but powerful, raising a farm from his bare hands in the Central Valley so the generations of his Filipino sons and daughters wouldn't have to go through what he did, for nothing. You see, I was raised to see not in moments but in histories. An hour ago I told my dad that I wasn't going to be premed anymore. And two weeks after this phone call I'll be in a Chem 33 final exam with pencil, paper, and calculator that are breaking under the pressure of my flood of sweat. I had a fear of squandering. Washing down drains. Tasting salt on my breath.

And so I remember my grandfather I never met. His stooped back was the archway that welcomed my dad to college. Am I sacrilege to the ruins?

Six months after this phone call I will be performing spoken word at the workers' rally at the four-way intersection on Palm Drive. I will humbly recite in solidarity with the women and men whose hands are deemed "unskilled" by the very academy that they keep alive. But in the pursuit of poetry over pediatrics, do I forget the martyrdom of my brown and weathered ancestry?

I remember. I question. I step forward and remember to look back. I understand that it's impossible to ever truly stand up alone.

Takeo Rivera 2008

I LIVE FOR CONVERSATIONS WRITTEN

and oral and everything in between. I live for the gasps you can read. The text you can smell. The living book of our collective authorship. Chapters carved on countenances. Love real and imagined. And the unremarkable, mundane stuff that we live in the oft-forgotten breaths we catch during each quarter. Lying in bed until the last possible moment to get to our morning classes. Baring our souls to friends at 2 a.m. Wondering during lecture about him or her or the other wonderful possibilities of being in one's early twenties and surrounded by others in their early twenties. And as wonderful and expansive and awe-inspiring as these moments are, I live to serve, hoping that my hands and conversations can somehow open up a world or two.

Takeo Rivera 2008

I WOULD LIKE TO MOVE YOU.

Someday.

M. O.
2009

I REMEMBER LONG SUMMERS

in the backyard with my sisters, tumbling in the grass and climbing trees and examining anything that we could find in the flowerbeds. I remember the foggy morning in third grade when, riding my bike to school, I ran into the back of a parked truck and the drizzly morning many years later when I crashed my dad's car into another stationary object, this time a wall. I remember the Wednesday in fourth grade that my parents pretended we were going to school, but took us to Disneyland instead. I remember how amazing home-cooked pasta tasted when I went back home for the first time after I started college.

M.O. 2009

I LIVE FOR THE THRILL OF STEPPING

on an airplane and knowing that I'll end up somewhere else. I live for having the window seat, and watching states and countries and oceans go by instead of watching whatever movie is on. I live for seeing the sun rise from thousands of miles above the ground, as the stars disappear and the clouds change from gray to purple to orange. I live for the bizarre convergence of a couple of hundred lives in a metal box, when no one knows anyone and the only way to learn about the other people is from what you see out of the corner of your eye, and whether they're drinking ginger ale or orange juice.

M.O. 2009

I WOULD LIKE TO SPEAK

several languages and live in several countries. I would like to find out what other people think about me, and tell everyone what I think about them. I would like to help people communicate better, whether the barrier is language, social conventions, fear, or anything else that can keep one person from giving another a chance. In the meantime, I'd like to figure out what my major is...

M.O. 2009

NATE DOWNS
2006

I REMEMBER BEING A FRESHMAN

on the gymnastics team. I was so amazed by how good and how tough all the upperclassmen were. It was crazy to go from the very top of my club team to the bottom ranks of the college team. It was my proving ground and I took the challenge of becoming worthy of competing for Stanford very seriously. It was also really cool to have a really cohesive team- in the past my gymnastics teams had been groups of individuals. This team was a solid unit and becoming a part of that greater group was a very powerful thing for me.

Nate Downs 2006

I LIVE FOR RIGHT NOW, MY LAST

last quarter of senior year, I live to make the most out of the end of my college experience. I want to look back on these years and smile when I remember how much fun I had with friends. I feel like so much of Stanford is so caught up in being smart and studying that they often lose sight of enjoying themselves. I know I've been like that in the past (I've had to be in order to be successful at both gymnastics and school).

Seriously, I've never seen at least half of the people who go to this school because it seems like they never leave their rooms. To those people, I say, "Get out of your room and enjoy this beautiful place we call school. Leave the books now and then and have some fun!" It seems like Stanford kids are growing smarter but becoming less well-rounded. To the incoming frosh classes, I say:

"Save some time for yourselves. Enjoy your time here so that you don't look back on this time with any regrets."

Nate Downs 2006

I WOULD LIKE TO:

Hit it big with my startup.
Pay off my ridiculous student loans.
Own a winery.
Contribute to the sustanability of
the human race on this planet.

MARISA DOWLING
2009

Marisa mis-interpreted the prompts and only wrote about one. However, her entry is so zesty and delightful that I had to include it. - Jason

I WOULD LIKE TO BE FREE.

If Life handed me a year of freedom (and a sizable amount of money), what would I not do?

January would equal R&R 101. Currently, my brain spends its time fluttering maddeningly around my body, attempting to build Rome in a day. Consequently, sleep and exercise fall last on my list of priorities. To dispel the situation, I would buckle down for a Disney movie marathon, revamp my outrageously out-dated web page, indulge in some quality family time, and exorcise the Chubby Demon by handing my soul over to a personal trainer. With all that in place, I could finally say, "Houston, we have nirvana."

Rejuvenated, I would sojourn briefly to Cozumel, Mexico and cry my eyes out, while swimming with the dolphins-- my childhood fantasy. Mid-February would find me globe-trotting across Greece, Rome, Paris, and Britain (with particular emphasis on all things Harry Potter), before exploring the soggy shores of the Emerald Isle in early May. Pausing for a bit, I would fill my

Marisa Dowling 2009

stomach with potatoes, while filling my head with intricate Irish dancing steps-- not that Riverdance stuff either. Oh no. Only real, wee-lass-with-red-hair-and-a-lacy-sash kind of dancing will do. Although not expecting to become a grand master, I hope to hop my way through at least a couple routines.

Next, Spain would serenade my heart, beckoning me to its arid plains. June through mid-September's agenda includes covering my eyes during a bull fight and siesta-ing in a cozy hacienda, sombrero tipped just right. Not liking just to observe, I would zealously apply for a job, submerging myself totally in the language. But staying in one place would hardly appease my wanderlust. To sate that appetite without moving would require nothing less than adrenaline-pumping, danger-ridden, traditional fencing lessons. With my deep ardor for the sport born of late night Zorro episodes, I fully expect to crush many a fool who would cross my path and maybe foil the evil plots of a greedy comandante.

With "Mission Sword Fluency" accomplished, I would then enlist in some charity organization, as I could not in good conscience spend an entire year selfishly satisfying my own fancies. Banking on my new Spanish skills, I would work in Central or South America, maybe even teaching English at a local school, while unearthing valuable lessons in culture and perspective.

Two weeks before the end of the year, I would return to the United States and savor a final thrill: skydiving, just to remind myself that life, like the jump, passes quickly, so I need to relish life while it lasts!

I am a person who knows how to dream. But more importantly, I am a person dedicated to those dreams. I leave mediocrity to those too afraid to aspire. Only the height of living will do for me. These adventures will come true. So next time you find yourself outside, look up. You may just spy me plunging towards you, screaming to my heart's content!

E. K.
2008

I REMEMBER THE TIME A PIANO

instructor told me that I would never make it at a competition, that I had no talent, and I was so crushed that I never wanted to play again. That year, I got a new teacher. I went to a nationwide competition. I won first place.

I remember the time when I was most depressed, and had the least amount of faith in myself, and yet I still had enough of me still kicking that I could honestly confront another girl who was always whining about her life when times weren't that hard. You know, I said, you let the universe beat you down. You lie in a corner and take it and bemoan your fate. When the universe beats me down, like it is doing now, I'll be damned if I don't punch it back in the face.

I remember the lovely lady who knit me a blanket made of the rainbow when I was twelve, a purple car driving me to school everyday, being kidnapped and driven to the cheesecake factory for my graduation present. I remember my mother crying when my aunt died, and laughing hysterically at my sister's antics. I remember the day I got into Stanford, and I asked, but why? I don't get it. Aren't they lying? I didn't understand why they would put 'congratulations' on the envelope. I thought they were trying to trick me. When I opened the letter, my mother picked up the congratulations envelope and chased me around the house hitting me with it.

E.K. 2008

I LIVE TO UNDERSTAND.

I live to know the best of people. I love watching people and trying to find out what they love most in their lives, what drives them. I live to know the best things about the world around me, how our thoughts are formed, what makes us happy, how different neural networks firing can change your outlook on life. How the world is composed from things as tiny but magnificent as quarks and leptons, that make up us and everything around us, and spread out as far as the galaxy.

I live for the ocean, being able to wash it crashing onto the sand and being able to love it for what it is. I live for my little nephews. I live for the moments when I'm not sure whether I'm in love with something or they've just stepped on my foot. I live for nerdy jokes. Like, "oooh you must be my sympathetic nervous system because you make my heart beat sooooo fast". I live for ridiculous people who climb through windows when they're drunk, are from Singapore. I like topis. I live for love and I live for life.

E.K. 2008

I WOULD LIKE TO MAKE A DIFFERENCE.

I want to discover how we learn, how to remedy the worst of depressions, how to help those who most need it. I want to fight against oppression, oversimplification, and misunderstandings. I want people, as well as me, to learn how to understand each other better. I want to go to my mother's home in Mumbai and work in the slums. I want to create ideas and innovations I've never dreamed of. I want to be a better person. And I want to spread happiness and calm wherever I go.

E.K. 2008

PETER DERMAN
2007

I REMEMBER TRAVELING

to what seemed like another planet. It was a vast desert, and I was in the Algerian Sahara. The ocean of golden sand dunes was punctuated by rust-colored stone outcroppings from which I could see for miles in all directions. Yet no matter where I turned, I saw the same alien landscape. My little sister and I would scramble to the top of the mountainous dunes and then roll all the way back down through the soft, powdery sand.

I recall that trip often as I study in my room, practice at the gym or work in the lab. I sometimes get so wrapped up in my activities that I forget the vast world around me. Those picturesque dunes sit there now as they did before, only I am on the other side of the world. It's a strange thought.

I LIVE TO BE HAPPY.

As far as I can tell, I only get to be alive once so I'd better not waste time on things I don't enjoy. I love to learn, exercise, enjoy the outdoors, and surround myself with interesting people. Oh, not to mention long, romantic walks on the beach.

Peter Derman 2007

I WOULD LIKE TO SAIL

across the Pacific. Go to medical school. Live on a boat. Become a world-renowned surgeon. Live in a modern house. Have a family. Live in New York. Live in California. Become the first Jewish kid elected Pope (yes, rather ambitious). Travel to Antarctica. Read as many books as possible. Be remembered for doing something great.

Peter Derman 2007

H. Z.
2009

I REMEMBER BEING A MATH NERD.

Oh, the glorious days of solving Rubik's cubes to the oohs and ahhs of my classmates, of suffering through six weeks of the worst "pork ribs" imaginable for the sake of understanding the culture of math camp. The next year, one more student from my high school went to math camp; my senior year, over ten applied. I remember the days when math camp wasn't yet cool, and only a select few of us understood how bad food changed lives

H.Z. 2009

I LIVE FOR ALL-NIGHTERS:

before exams, after formals, and especially during The Game. The Game found me at South San Francisco at 9:00 pm, Fisherman's Wharf at 2:00 am, IHOP at 6:00 am, and spending all the pms and ams I could want in a car with four other puzzle lovers and $50 worth of unhealthy snacks from Safeway. A Stanford experience? I can't think of any better.

H.Z. 2009

I WOULD LIKE TO SEE AN OPERA

at the Metropolitan Opera in New York, see a Chekhov play put on in Russia, maybe see a giant squid at the bottom of the ocean. I would like to change the world, but in my free time, I'd settle for seeing the world. The afternoons spent reading news articles on the Internet and novels on my bed will one day find their purpose, when I show up in St. Petersburg and exclaim, "Hey! That's the statue that Dostoevsky passed every day when he was writing *The Brothers Karamazov*!"

H.Z. 2009

N. J.
2008

I   REMEMBER

dressing up as ghosts
with my grandfather and
scaring my sister.

I   LIVE   FOR

the silence of friends
and sake of others.

I WOULD LIKE TO

retire early and forget about
the money.

STEDMAN WILSON
2006

I   REMEMBER   FRESHMAN   YEAR,

from the initial feeling of achievement and excitement to attend Stanford University, to the abrupt transition of life away from home, and finally to the personal discovery that came from choosing a major. I must have juggled ten different major ideas, from computer science, to symbolic systems, to music, to physics and math. I chose physics, and I haven't regretted it since.

I remember sitting in an auditorium at the end of freshman year, listening to a talk given by Mathematica creator Steven Wolfram about his newly published book, *A New Kind of Science*. I spent the following summer reading that book. That was one of the most intellectually exciting things I have ever experienced.

I remember my community service group Young at Heart (now Side by Side). Comprised of the eighteen nicest people I've ever met, Young at Heart was a defining part of my first two years at Stanford. Young at Heart taught me how to sing and perform as part of a group, and how to reach out to others. And singing grade-A material from the big band and doo-wop eras--it doesn't get much better than that.

I remember the Institute. By which I mean the Institute for the Advancement of Funk and Soul. We were also a community service group, of sorts. But more than that, we were the funkiest function ever to hit Stanford campus. I remember late night band practices until 3 AM in Braun music center. I remember locking ourselves out of the building with all our music equipment locked inside. And most of all, I remember driving our guitarist's roomate's golf cart to and from row houses, packed full of instruments and amps. It's a long way to the top, if you want to rock.

Stedman Wilson 2006

I LIVE FOR MUSIC AND MATH.

I've played music since I was little. And more than ever, for the past three years I've been a man on a mission. The mission: to achieve proficiency on three musical instruments. Sound like mission impossible? Well, honestly I've felt the same way more times than I can recall. But something kept me going. What was it? What is it about music that makes one feel he can conquer his fears and live his dreams?

I have not majored in music, but through all my work and all my play, music has remained a backdrop--through music I tell my story. It gets me through the bad times and the good. But music is more than that. It is a starting point--a schedule that shapes my day, and a vision that shapes my goals.

If there is one unifying force among my academic passions, it's math. If you're like me, you believe that everything can be explained by math, from quark interactions all the way up to politics and love. If that's not beautiful, I don't know what is. This is what I live for. Understanding, and the pursuit of knowledge. Discovering secrets in hidden places--that's a joy even big kids can relate to.

Stedman Wilson 2006

I WOULD LIKE TO FIND A THEORY

of everything. A year ago I sat down and wrote out a shabby, home-grown website in a unix-based text editor--it was the site of a project, that began simply as a way for me to organize my thoughts and knowledge about life, the universe, and everything. But could it ever be more than that? One day, I would like to see this site become the homepage of an actual initiative, discovering new principles and providing ever sharper insight into the unifying fabric that connects our lives and our minds. A theory of everything? Everything I learn puts me one step closer.

L. G.
2008

I REMEMBER LEARNING HOW TO PLAY

pool in my grandma's basement when I was five. Her basement served as a bar/party room and it was probably around midnight. As I later learned, everyone was completely inebriated and found the little curly-haired girl peering over the edge of the pool table trying to hit the ball (and failing miserably) rather entertaining. When I grew tired of pool I sat behind the bar and played bartender to the party-goers. At the ripe age of five I learned how to make a potently delicious irish coffee from my life-of-the-party grandma. Classic, elegant, and stunning, she sat on a stool next to me and made me feel like I was the only person in the world who mattered. Whether she was slipping me chocolate candy late at night against my mom's wishes, buying me poofy and sparkly dresses because I adored tacky clothes, or just letting me crawl into bed with her in the mornings while she said her prayers, when she was around there was never a doubt in my mind that I was loved. That was her gift and something I strive to live up to everyday.

L.G. 2008

I LIVE FOR TAKING NAPS.

I nap after class and before practice in the afternoons because I woke up at 5:45 am for morning workouts. I nap before going to the library to work because I am exhausted from practice. I nap before going out on the weekends because I am so tired from staying up to finish problem sets due at the end of the week. I nap in between games of soccer tournaments. Basically, naps save my life because without them I would be dangerously sleep deprived.

L.G. 2008

I WOULD LIKE TO

attend a FIFA World Cup Final.

A. P.
2009

I REMEMBER WHEN I WAS IN FIRST GRADE,

we had to make our own spelling tests. I would look for the biggest words I could find, because I didn't want to learn how to spell "cat" for another week. I got made fun of for trying too hard. I remember when I moved to the US and saw my mom crying because the principal of the school wouldn't let my brother and I take an entrance exam because she believed that schools in Mexico and Brazil were not up to par.

I remember getting into that school.

I remember leaving it and skipping a grade at my next school. I remember going through the troubling middle school years as the awkward girl who actually wore shorts of the required length for her uniform and did all her homework. I remember being on the varsity team while in middle school. I remember having very few friends. I remember being rejected for a scholarship at that school, and moving on to a public high school.

I remember feeling lost and alone for a few days. I remember finding my circle of friends, joining clubs, becoming active, and having a dream. I remember filling out my college applications, and stressing about deadlines. I remember being confused about where I would end up, and the weight of the decision killing me. And then I remember crying when I got the Stanford envelope. I remember walking around the Oval during Admit weekend and telling my dad...I'm coming to Stanford.

A.P. 2009

I LIVE FOR MY FAMILY, FOR MY FRIENDS,

and for humanity. I live to preserve the wonders we have and to improve what we can. I live to be a part of a community fueled with love and compassion, not by greed.

A.P. 2009

I WOULD LIKE BE AN ENGINEER.

I would like to save the planet. I would like to start a non-profit. I would like to do anything and everything I can to help people. As an engineer my passion for technology is rooted in making it compatible with our environment. I want to induce strength in every individual, I want to provide all people with the opportunities I had, because what I've had is beautiful.

A.P. 2009

M. A. K.
2008

I REMEMBER RUNNING AWAY FROM

crazy little girls in grade school. I remember leaving that school to go to a school where my parents thought I could get a better education. I remember making some really good friends for years to come and leaving others behind. I remember playing for the conference championship in soccer my senior year. I remember forcing myself through swimming even though I hated the incredibly intense workouts. I remember being a part of the best volleyball team ever. I remember dancing on stage as a part of the Latino Club. I remember making some great friends that I will keep in touch with the rest of my life. I met the girl of my dreams and I got into the school of my dreams. And still it seems the best is yet to come.

M.A.K. 2008

I LIVE TO MAKE CLOSE FRIENDS

that you can always count on. I live for the long car rides you take with those friends to random places just for fun.

I live to play volleyball, whether on the sand or in the gym. I live for the feeling of having helped someone solve a problem that has been bothering them for sometime. I live for the many unknowns the future holds.

M.A.K. 2008

I WOULD LIKE TO MAKE IT THROUGH

college without any regrets because I had made the most of the experience. I would like to get a job in an industry that will allow me to live comfortably. I would like to work at a job I love. I would like to remain close with my family even after I go off on my own to start my own family. I would like to be happy.

M.A.K. 2008

LEAH SAWYER
2007

I REMEMBER THE FIRST TIME I RACED

in a Stanford uniform. At first, the skimpy buns and unfamiliar singlet seemed like pieces out of a dress up wardrobe. My fellow freshmen and I spent a good portion of the night laughing in front of the mirror and posing for pictures that we then thought were ridiculous. Now, the Stanford uniform is my second skin. Every time I run in cardinal red I am reminded that the effort I put out on that day represents more than myself; it represents my teamates, the teamates before me, and the Stanford Tradition of excellence. Pictures of my classmates in those uniforms are no longer tinged with absurdity, but are documentations of records broken, championships won, and performances that shatter the mere notion of limitation.

I LIVE FOR CREATIVITY

and independence. I live for the ability
to create or accomplish something
completely my own, and the ability to
witness such creations by others. I live for
the ability to strive, to strain, and to stress
because that ability is a reward in itself,
and the creation a motivation to pursue
further goals.

Leah Sawyer 2007

I WOULD LIKE TO FIND HAPPINESS

through my work. Like all humans, I am not immune to future dreams of love, marriage, family, and security. Yet my distinct dream is to truly excel in the occupation of physical therapy, passionately provide services to others, and continue to learn and improve until the day I retire.

Leah Sawyer 2007

ABBY ZEITLIN
2008

I REMEMBER WHEN I WENT FISHING

with my mom and sister in Mexico. As a protest against my father, my mother decided to take the two girls out and show them how to deep-sea fish. She woke us up at 4:00 am and my sister and I dutifully waded out to the ponga where two skuzzy fishermen awaited us. We tried to catch fish for six hours, but the only things we caught were a decent case of seasickness, the sun, and some sea salt.

After six hours, the fishermen drove us over a reef, dropped three fishing poles in the water and told us to start fishing. We submitted, took the poles and in no time caught a fish; a puffer fish. It came up flat, puffed out once it reached the surface, then stole the hook. And, finally my mom was ready. We all took the anti-fishing vow: Never again would the women of my family attempt to deep-sea fish.

I LIVE FOR THE HEAT.

There is something exciting about getting out of my air-conditioned car into 100 degree heat. It's that initial shock of dizziness and then realization, that somehow, some way I will make it through the fatal heat to the next air-conditioned destination. Safe at a last from the deadly claws that try to grip at life.

Abby Zeitlin 2008

I WOULD LIKE TO LAY FOR ONE FULL DAY

in the grass in the oval and just stare at the sky. I would like to walk the Appalachian Trail. I would like to participate in a reenactment of the Civil War.

Abby Zeitlin 2008

MARIBEL DIAZ
2008

I REMEMBER THE SUNRAYS PEAKING

from the dark skies as my dad took my twin sister and I to the swap meet in the wee hours of the morning to secure a good spot for my mother to sell clothes for the day. It was an adventure as I would sleep in the back of the car seat and be rewarded with donut holes for being a good girl. Life was rough back then but I was fortunately too young to realize that. My parents were following the American Dream and were struggling in the land of opportunity to provide a better life for their three daughters (and future son). It was worth it.

Fast forward thirteen years later to December 12, 2004. I remember arriving early to home from school. There was a twinkle in my parents' eyes as I entered the door, and my attention shifted to the mail. Sitting on the table was not one but TWO Stanford acceptances. Both my twin sister and I had been accepted early to Stanford.

Ultimately, I was the only one who chose Stanford and on the ride up north for NSO wrapped up in my fluffy pink bathrobe since I was not aware of the chilly weather up North. I cried until I was no longer able to. I cried for the friends I left behind, the scent of my mom's kitchen when she was cooking, and many other things I would miss. But most of all, I cried for my twin sister since I knew I would not see her again until Christmas.

Now that I am finishing my second year at Stanford, these memories seem very distant but I will remember them always.

Maribel Diaz 2008

I LIVE TO BRING JOY TO THE LIFE OF OTHERS.

A small note or thank you always goes a long way and is greatly appreciated. I smile incessantly and love to laugh as it not only brightens my day but I know it also affects those around me.

I live to enjoy life, and learn from those around me! There is so much to do and life passes by so fast it's hard to stop and take it all in. Sometimes as I bike across the main quad during spring quarter, I pause to admire the beauty of nature. In regard to individuals, Stanford has taught me how unique and talented everyone is. Every person has their own story, and I am left speechless by how much everyone has to offer.

Finally, I live to grow in my Christian faith. It is an important part of who I am, and it is one of the main things that keep me going when I want to give up. Also, it is the one thing in my life that I do not have to leave behind when life takes directs me to a new path.

Maribel Diaz 2008

I WOULD LIKE TO BE HAPPY

with my career choice (whatever this may be!). I may not know where my interests and passions will lead, but I am certain that I will not regret it. I would like to live a simple life that is not bogged down by unnecessary distractions. Above all, I hope I am given health and am always surrounded by those who love me.

As random as this may sound, I would like to become a cake decorator extraordinaire. I dream of learning how to recreate the gorgeous frosted delicacies I have seen in magazines, books, and stores. I want to master the art of making fondant petals, luscious butter cream roses, or chocolate shavings.

Maribel Diaz 2008

JASON SHEN
2008

I REMEMBER LONG, SWEATY PRACTICES,

starting homework at 10PM and dreaming of snow in the morning. I remember feeling so trusted when my cat would fall asleep on my lap. I remember playing with my baby sister and thinking she had to be absolute cutest thing on earth.

I remember my mom running into school to tell me I had gotten into to Stanford. I remember her crying when I first had to leave. I remember the exhilaration of freshman year, the isolation of sophomore year and I feel anticipation for many years to come.

I am always envious of people who recall events in the past with great clarity. It seems that I can only remember song lyrics, commercials, and random articles I've read online. At the end of my life I figure I can spit back half of wikipedia, but not remember my wedding, birth of my child or what I did to win my Nobel Peace Prize (I'm only half kidding).

Well, that's why journals, digital cameras and yearbooks were invented. To help us remember. They say the older you get, the more you need people who knew you when you were young. If that's's true for most people, it'll be 10 times as true for me.

Hey what did we do at Stanford again?

Jason Shen 2008

I LIVE TO SHARE INSIGHT.

I live to improve myself and improve the lives of others.   I live to laugh, (and I guess I live to cry, although it happens rarely because I seem to be one of those people who is positive nearly all the time).

I know I have but one life and I intend to live it to the fullest. I live for a better tomorrow.

Jason Shen 2008

I WOULD LIKE TO DO SO MANY THINGS,

it's not even funny. I would like to win an NCAA Team Championship. I want that big fat ring so bad.

I would like to spend a year learning things that were not fully addressed in my formal education. I'd travel around the world, take pictures, read books and meet interesting and exciting people.

I would like to write books - fantasy novels, space operas, memoirs, comic books, manifestos about saving the world, and collections of thoughts from great and inspired minds.

I would like to raise a family. I'd like to have a child and adopt one. Knowing what I know about biology, my kids are going to be super amazing.

I am an idealist, I know. But I am a commited idealist. And a smart one. And a caring one. I don't know how I will do it just yet, but I would like to, and I will, make significant and positive contributions towards life on this planet through my intelligence, drive and compassion.

Jason Shen 2008

ANONYMOUS
200?

I REMEMBER BEING ONE OF TWO GIRLS

to cross the line when asked if we thought we were proud of our looks. I looked around and remember being confused as to why everyone else was not proud of themselves. I remember feeling sad because everyone is so pretty and good looking and they don't realize it.

I remember my first time cooking for 40 people at Hammarskjold and how my dinner was 30 minutes late and the chicken was still pink.

I remember clambering over rocks and bushes to get to the sulphur hot springs in Big Sur, and I remember the skinny dipping that ensued. I remember one friend running into the cold river naked. I remember him returning to the hot springs saying the river took away his glasses. I remember having to lead him back to camp in the dark and over those rocks (fully clothed).

I remember standing on a frozen and snow covered lake in Desolation Wilderness with snowshoes bound on my feet. I remember lying in a snow cave (aka the love den) and seeing the gorgeous green blue of ice as the sun hit the walls of snow from above.

I remember floating upside down in the pool with a dry suit on and trying to do a somersault under water to kick my floating legs under me. I remember floating to the top of the water with air still in my legs. The next day I remember doing a somersault in the sea waters of Monterey as sea otters and seals played around me.

Anonymous 200?

I LIVE TO ENJOY THE BEAUTIFUL SUN

and be continually kissed by its friendly rays. I live to explore the blue planet we call the ocean and continue to search for why God would create such amazing creatures under the water where no human is meant to see them. I live for those nudibranchs and purple and gold spiralled shelled slugs. I live to find all the amazing people in this world and read the storybook they call their lives. I live to encounter a spectrum of people that color this mundane world with their oddities, normalities, extremities, and quirks. I live for myself to enjoy this life I have been given to the fullest. I live to challenge myself, be challenged, and challenge others to be the person we want to be.

Anonymous 200?

I WOULD LIKE TO SLOWLY BUT SURELY

change the world by doing good (and by first of all not doing harm). I will affect lives and be affected through person to person exchange. I would like to see more people in this world be as united, loving, and carefree as my beloved Hammarskjold I have lived in. I would like to see the world be filled with "win win" situations and be witness to the powerful forces of synergy. I would like to have more Cafe Nights in my life where tables are meant to be danced on and music is meant to be danced to.

Anonymous 200?

*Are you a Stanford student who wants to write for **Stanford Spirit 2?***

*Check out **www.stanfordspirit.com** for more information.*

New prompts.
New voices.